The Power of the Commentariat

How much do commentators influence politics and public opinion?

A report by Julia Hobsbawm and John Lloyd

Published by Editorial Intelligence Ltd in association
with the Reuters Institute for the Study of Journalism.
Publishing partners: Weber Shandwick and
City of London Corporation.

Published by Editorial Intelligence Ltd in association with the
Reuters Institute for the Study of Journalism.
Publishing partners: Weber Shandwick and
City of London Corporation.
Copyright Julia Hobsbawm and John Lloyd 2008

Case Study Research: Sophie Radice
Copy editor: Sarah Benton and Francesca Spickernell
Interview Co-ordinator: Caroline Fielding
Design: O'Mara

WEBER SHANDWICK

CITY
OF
LONDON

ISBN 978-0-9559103-0-2

CONTENTS

Acknowledgments   6

Introduction   7

Humble journalist: the commentators' self-image   9

Power in the eye of the beholder: our poll findings   15

The daily grind: what do commentators do?   18

   i.   Entertain   18

   ii. Set agendas   20

   iii. Tell the truth   21

   iv. Do battle   22

   v. Spot and set trends   23

   vi. Address constituencies   23

   vii. Change minds and hearts (their own)   24

   viii. Make or break reputations   25

Hug your enemy very close: managing the commentariat   26

Rising tide of opinion: broadcast v print v blogs   28

Conclusion   33

Number crunching: Editorial Intelligence case studies   34

Index   45

Biographies

Julia Hobsbawm

Julia Hobsbawm is Founder and Chief Executive of the media analysis and networking firm Editorial Intelligence Ltd. She is Visiting Professor of Public Relations at the London College of Communication, University of the Arts, and is the editor of *Where the Truth Lies: Trust & Morality in PR and Journalism*. Her book about work-life balance, called *The See-Saw*, will be published in 2009 by Atlantic Books.

John Lloyd

John Lloyd is the co-founder and director of journalism at the Reuters Institute for the Study of Journalism at the University of Oxford, a Contributing Editor of the Financial Times and a member of the editorial board of Prospect Magazine. His books include Rebirth of a Nation: *An Anatomy of Russia* (1998) and *What the Media Are Doing to our Politics* (2004). He has won four national journalism awards for his journalism.

Acknowledgments

We are equally grateful to those who gave their time in person, and by email, telephone, and online survey for this report. Caroline Fielding deserves special thanks for patiently co-ordinating all the interviews. Limits on length prevent us from quoting everyone, and from those we do quote, at the length we might like. We are grateful to the researchers and analysts at Editorial Intelligence and Editor Stephen Fleming and Editorial Director Charlie Burgess: the hundreds of thousands of words of summarised comment, interpreted by Sophie Radice, provide our detailed research at the end of this report. Without the rising significance of the flourishing wit and wisdom of Britain's commentators and bloggers this report would, of course, not have been possible at all.

Julia Hobsbawm and John Lloyd
London April 2008.

The Power of the Commentariat

British commentators usually disclaim much influence. As Jackie Ashley of The Guardian put it in mid-April, 2008: "we columnists are just fleas on the body politic". Few of those to whom we spoke would allow their or their fellows' writing more than a modest importance – and even that was said to be elusive as to evidence, with "anecdotal" being the most common response to a question on how they knew they had any effect.

But it is balanced by another, opposing belief – that is, that journalists in general and commentators in particular follow the injunction apocryphally attributed to the 17th century Quaker George Fox: "speak truth to power". Many of those to whom we spoke strongly believed that was their mission in life – yet some of these who did also said that they believed that their work had no intrinsic importance.

This dichotomy runs through not just the minds of journalists : it is inherent in the nature of the commentators' trade. It is true that it is, like most journalism, transient: and it is true that it must catch the wandering attention, a task more difficult now because of a vast array of media and other competitors for time and interest. But it is also the case that British newspaper commentary is among the liveliest, most combative and sharpest in the world; that it is now seen by editors and owners of newspapers as more important than reporting, at least as measured in the amount of money paid to commentators as against that paid to reporters and the privileging of commentators on the skylines of newspapers. Further, and most importantly in this context, most of those within political life see political columns as of fundamental importance to the conduct of their public lives.

British columnists are, in the main, independent, or certainly regard themselves as such. In many, perhaps most, cultures of journalism in the world the commentator speaks for – and is more or less explicitly paid to speak for – the state, or a corporation, or a party, or a powerful individual. In Britain, both the virtual and literal coin of the commentators' trade is at least apparent independence. To be seen to speak for an entity more powerful than the commentator is to court ridicule from colleagues and a fall in worth in the eyes of the readers. It may well be – it usually is – that the commentator's views accord at least roughly with those of his newspaper's editor and editorial position. Howell James, the Permanent Secretary, Government Communications, at the Cabinet Office, said that newspapers had become "more of a seamless whole these days – there aren't many differing voices within them."

There is a gorgeousness about a columnist who represents a political dogma; it's almost a form of integrity

– Peter Oborne

Polly Toynbee of The Guardian dissents from the view that commentators are independent. Though she agrees with Howell James that, as she says: "Commentators reflect in the main the positions that most of their papers take," she nevertheless adds that, therefore, "most commentators are on the right because that's the way the British press is. Columnists like (Richard) Littlejohn, (Trevor) Kavannagh and (Melanie) Phillips are influential because they go with the grain of their owners, and their owners – especially Rupert Murdoch - are powerful" . But most – certainly the three Toynbee mentions – would argue that their views are their own, even if a newspaper, or a proprietor, hired them to give them. The columnist Mary Riddell, who writes for the Daily Telegraph, said that she wished never to be so close to anyone to whom she spoke that she felt constrained to "write anything that you don't wholly believe". And this independence of thought gives commentators a good deal of power. Politicians are often accused of being 'on message' as a sign of obeisance before the party whips. No commentator worth their salt wishes to have such a charge laid at their door: their personal opinions, or what are taken to be their personal opinions, are their currency.

Humble journalist:
commentator self-image

No commentator to whom we spoke said s/he was powerful.
It doesn't figure on the permissible responses of British commentators.
The columnist who said this most strongly was Peter Oborne of the
Daily Mail (whose weekly column is sub-titled "On politics and power"):
"I don't agree with the premise that the commentariat is powerful.
I broadly think it is hard to see examples of it having any effect at all.
I only have in mind the readers. I don't have any power at all."

When pushed, some would say their writing might have swayed opinions.
Melanie Phillips of the Daily Mail said that her warnings on the threat of
militant Islam – especially her book, "Londonistan" – might have convinced
civil servants that it was a more serious problem than they had believed; Nick
Cohen of the Observer and London's Evening Standard thought his columns
on the same subject might have had the same effect. Outside of politics,
commentators on business and economics make similar points, usually
denying any direct, evidential influence but – as Stefan Stern, who writes a
management column for the FT, states: "It contributes to debate: it can start
debate off…a handful of superstar columnists could no doubt point to
significant changes in policy or approach". Iain Martin of the Telegraph

**" I would like to think that my refusal to accept that cannabis was
a safe, soft drug - when all around were falling for the dope
propagandists - has made it easier for politicians to backtrack on
the legal downgrading of marijuana"** – Peter Hitchens

Media Group said that he, and other commentators of the centre-right,
probably did have some influence in the Cameron shadow cabinet because
they were, as oppositions usually are, in the stage of looking for new
approaches and ideas and look to find them from commentators among
others; and as we will see, commentators are seen, and seen by themselves, as
moving opinions in certain circumstances. Suzanne Moore of the Mail on
Sunday said: "Politicians are loath to admit that they are influenced but they
do badger my editor to get rid of me or shut me up, or try to take me out to
lunch". Gideon Rachman, the foreign affairs columnist on the FT, says: "I
don't see myself as influencing people. In fact, I don't want a chap in
Whitehall or the White House changing his view because of what I write. I

want to set people thinking – that's all".

On the other hand…Polly Toynbee says that her writing on the Sure Start programme and other social issues probably did help – in that it supported those ministers who were for the programme to press on with it. "Ministers said it helped: I think it helped people to go on who were going that way anyway. It helped in that, unlike most commentators who come from covering politics or sometimes economics, I come from a social affairs background – reporting on policy issues, not on performance of the ministers." Martin Wolf, of the Financial Times, is the one of our interviewees who protests no modesty, false or otherwise: he believes that the FT is uniquely influential among newspapers – not just in the UK, but in the world, an influence deriving from its elite readership, its global span and what he calls its "open-mindedness", that is, a reputation for examining issues on their strengths and weaknesses, not conforming to a pre-determined ideological stance. "I think I did have some influence on a particular issue - that of university fees (he was for them). I was told by Andrew Adonis (the Education Minister) that he had used my arguments with Tony Blair, and they had assisted in changing policy. And I think my work on globalisation (Wolf wrote a book, *Why Globalisation Works*, and often deals with global economic issues in his column) had an effect, but mainly in supporting views which are pretty widely held among the elites". Timothy Garton Ash, the Oxford Professor of European Studies and regular Guardian columnist, said: "I don't think seeking to influence is the first reason one writes. The first reason is to write something true and interesting. Second, it is to speak to your readers. And third, it is to perhaps influence government and other actors. I hate the "memo to the President" columns: readers are, in the main, not the President."

Many commentators believed they get what power they had from the relatively powerless – that is, the readers. This is – perhaps naturally at the time of a centre-left Labour government – most strongly believed by commentators on the right. Melanie Phillips, the Daily Mail columnist whose blog was bought up by The Spectator and is now published exclusively online by www.spectator.co.uk , was among those to whom we talked who believed this most strongly. Her first declaration was that "I am not writing for people in power or for the media class – but for ordinary people…I've noticed that, over the years, large numbers of people will say – you must keep on; we are voiceless." Denise

> **"Shifting the discourse is what a good column should do. But I think we are leaving something out here which is the ability to entertain. We are not writing policy documents"**
>
> – Suzanne Moore

Kingsmill, the former chairman of the Competition Commission, says that financial commentators have most power when they connect with the concerns of shareholders – the business equivalent of the electorate. "Corporate leaders are not elected – but this is the constituency to which they are responsible, and feel most vulnerable".

A variation of the theme of powerlessness is that commentators are powerful only within the political/journalists' class – attended to only "inside the M25". Both the former European Minister Denis MacShane MP (whose parliamentary constituency is in Scunthorpe) and the head of the Press Complaints Commission (and former UK ambassador to Washington) Sir Christopher Meyer, said that they rarely heard any mention of the issues which obsess those, whom Editorial Intelligence calls the "Commentariat," outside London. This chimes in with another piece of commentators' self-denigration; that they are an overwhelmingly London-based elite, often living in pleasant and expensive parts of north and west London. Stefan Stern

"Because politicians spend time reading all this bollocks, comment is influential... ideally you don't want them reading the papers because it affects their vanity"
– Charlie Whelan

(albeit a South Londoner) said: "I sometimes think: who am I to tell people what's good and not good?" As Rachel Johnson of the Sunday Times put it: "In the end I'm a posh woman from Notting Hill."

The debate on degrees of powerlessness is not confined to the commentators, of course. At one extreme, Christopher Meyer believes very strongly that politicians should not confer on their commentator-tormentors any power whatsoever – a view he holds so passionately that he devoted much of our interview to it. Meyer had spent the first half of the 1990s as press spokesman to the then Prime Minister John Major and says: "I tried constantly to convince him not to read the newspapers and get upset with the commentators it never worked." He says: "The power of the commentators has been very much exaggerated, both by themselves and by the politicians. Politicians can react to the supposed power of the commentariat with craven obsequiousness. Both government departments and Number 10 have created very large staffs of press officers – one of the largest reasons for that is to influence the commentators. But in the end the power is slight. John Major was destroyed, not by the press, but by the European Exchange Rate Mechanism."

On the other side, the former cabinet minister Charles Clarke says: "Of course the commentariat is powerful. Any government committed to change needs to understand that the case for change can only be sustained through strong argument. Commentators reflect the strength of that argument. When I was Secretary of State for Education, driving through the bill on university tuition fees, a key strategic priority was to persuade a large variety of commentators of our argument. Because comment is a key conduit for arguments – not just the political theatre of the sketchwriters. They give intellectual underpinning and create intellectual fashion. Comment is the essential intersection between the political class and the public". Timothy Garton Ash gives some examples of where he thought he had influence: the clearest, he thought, was when he wrote in a signed Spectator column, and in an anonymous Times leader in 1984, that the then junior Foreign Minister, Malcolm Rifkind, should insist on visiting the grave of the recently murdered (by the secret police) priest, Jerzy Popieluszko on a visit to Poland. Because Garton Ash wrote two pieces – one by-lined, one not – "Rifkind must have felt there was a crescendo of opinion calling for him to visit the grave! And he did, to the fury of the Communists. So I think there was a bats' squeak of influence." Otherwise, he said, any influence is mostly diffuse and difficult to track

In an unusual exchange in April 2006 in the Observer, the columnist and Vanity Fair London Editor Henry Porter and the then Prime Minister Tony Blair set out their opposing views of the state of civil liberties. The fact that this exchange took place, and with such prominence on the opinion pages, speaks strongly for the power of the commentariat. Porter had been writing for some time about the erosion of civil liberties. He claimed that civil liberties in the UK were being destroyed in pursuit of security, ending his philippic with: "You have offered us a trade-off between freedom and security; I fear we will lose both." Blair replied by saying that much of what Porter wrote was "in the realm of fantasy" or simply incorrect.

In a parallel move, the then Home Secretary Charles Clarke wrote a letter responding to a column on April 15, 2006, by the Independent's Simon Carr (which began: "If you think you live in a liberal and democratic society, then please read on,") arguing that Carr had made a "series of incorrect, tendentious and over-simplified assertions about this government's record on civil liberties." He ended by saying that the "conclusion would be too much to ask of the 'Independent' newspaper." The Independent's "viewspaper" style of journalism, in which the reportage and the comment merge into each other and are both continually and highly critical of the government, irks politicians. Tony Blair singled the paper out for criticism in the speech he gave to the Reuters Institute in June 2007.

Senior politicians and other public figures emphasise the significance of the commentariat by becoming commentators themselves to create maximum impact. In the first four months of the year, leading politicians, including the Prime Minister Gordon Brown; the Leader of the Opposition David Cameron; the Foreign Secretary David Miliband; and the London Mayoral candidates Ken Livingstone, Boris Johnson; and Brian Paddick the Shadow Chancellor, all set out their political stall with by-lined comment pieces in the coveted 'guest' slots of the opinion pages of, amongst others, the Financial Times, the Sunday Times, the Guardian, Evening Standard and the News of the World. Business leaders join in: Justin King, chief executive of

Sainsbury's, complemented a broadcast think piece for the BBC's Newsnight on the use of plastic bags with a "Personal View" piece in the Daily Telegraph in April, defending his company's policy on plastic bags against that of the government.

Significantly, the "Thunderer" rubric – an appellation of the 19th century when it was coined to describe the influence of The Times' leaders – now serves as a signpost to guest columnists who "thunder" about this or that. Guest columnists themselves can be very powerful; indeed, the success of many comment pages is the calibre of their guest writers, and their topicality. Catherine Meyer, London bureau chief of Time magazine, mentioned Gloria Steinem and Caroline Kennedy, who both wrote guest op-ed pieces in favour of each Democratic candidate during critical stages in the primaries as being influential.

Howell James, who had senior roles as a political aide in 10 Downing Street and running public affairs for the BBC before becoming Permanent Secretary for Government Communications says. "Having worked closely with politicians for the last few years, I can see why they invest so much time to get on the right side of commentators. They want to set the context, and to demonstrate that they're on top of their job and making the right kind of waves. If you're in public life you can't afford to ignore the media."

The latter views seem to be dominant within politics itself, and among those who are close to the political scene. Matthew Taylor, the former head of the No 10 Policy Unit under Tony Blair, now chief executive of the Royal Society for the encouragement of Arts, Manufactures & Commerce (RSA)

"We do take a close interest in what the commentators are saying, but not necessarily more than the news pages. If we do, it is to find out who they have been speaking to, because generally it can only be one of around thirty five people" – anonymous Ministerial aide

said that Blair would read, and at times be swayed by, a selection of commentators who he though had some intellectual status. Charlie Whelan, the former press advisor to Gordon Brown in the early days of the latter's time at the Treasury, said: "Comment is hugely important because politicians read all this bollocks…ideally you don't want them reading the papers because it affects their vanity…politicians care what they say because people care what the commentators say". A senior aide to a cabinet minister, who would only speak on terms of anonymity, said; "Sensible cabinet ministers see the commentators as one part of a broad and diverse media mix, not the only part. They are valuable to help ministers hear what different voices in the country are saying, but the risk is that the purely political commentators, like Peter Riddell of the Times, are writing only for the Westminster square mile, and to have influence in comment you must get outside the sealed bubble of insiders and among the voters. To that extent the more mainstream commentators, like Richard Littlejohn in the Daily Mail, matter more because they write about issues like the Ghurkhas or police pay, which resonate with voters".

Ian Wylie, the CEO of the autism charity, TreeHouse Trust, says: "It seems there is no doubt that by-lined commentators have authority. They are read and their comments are critically scrutinised by a large majority of the people whose collective efforts go to shape policy and practice. Specifically...I think the commentariat has had an impact on the Brown government, which through a combination of inexperience and lack of directive leadership, has given a great deal of authority to commentators by paying them more attention than is perhaps healthy." In the business world, according to Denise Kingsmill, the effect of columns is undoubted – but mainly affects presentation rather than strategy. "It takes time for the effect to be felt – but one example is corporate social responsibility, where the press I believe played a big role in its encouragement. But it's undefined: there are movements and attitudes which change over time, in which the media play a major part." And Denis MacShane says: "Commentators' independence gives them power: "To paraphrase, facts are boring, comment is fun."

However, the political insiders insist – and the commentators do not, at least, demur – that ministers will follow unpopular courses of action, against even a united front of commentators, if they believe it right and if the Prime Minister and their senior colleagues are with them. Howell James said: "When ministers believe they have a strong case for something, even when it won't be popular and will be difficult to get through, they usually decide to go ahead, even against the commentariat."

"Educated middle-class people are fantastically impressionable. I believe I could change the minds of most of them with a column, or a dinner party conversation"

- Peter York

Power in the Eye of the Beholder:

Our Poll Results

As part of our research for this report we invited a self-selecting, small group of interested individuals from politics, business, media, public life, academia, and the more general reach of a group on Facebook set up by Editorial Intelligence called 'Keep up with the Commentariat' to tell us who they think are the most influential commentators, and generally how they rate the lie of the land between leader pages and columnists themselves.

What was most revealing about the findings is that media on both the left and right of the spectrum are deemed to be highly influential. So while Polly Toynbee of the Guardian consistently came top as the most influential commentator in the UK – polling nearly 70% of the vote - the Daily Mail followed by the Sun were counted as having the most influential leader columns.

Given that our poll coincided with a worsening economic outlook and daily headlines about mortgage rates, interest rates and 'the credit crunch' we were not surprised to see that out of top ten commentators listed, half are business and finance commentators: Irwin Stelzer of the Sunday Times, Martin Wolf of the Financial Times , Anatole Kaletsky of the Times, Robert Peston of the BBC whose business blog 'Peston's Picks' is one of the highest-ranked BBC blogs was rated equal 7th place with his predecessor as BBC Business Editor Jeff Randall, for his business column in the Daily Telegraph.

Commentators

Top Ten 'highly' influential commentators:

1. Polly Toynbee
2. Trevor Kavanagh
3. Irwin Stelzer
4. Nick Robinson
5. Anatole Kaletsky
6. Simon Jenkins
7. Robert Peston and Jeff Randall
8. Richard Littlejohn
9 George Monbiot
10. Martin Wolf and Matthew d'Ancona

Three of the most influential commentators: Nick Robinson of the BBC, Trevor Kavanagh of the Sun and Matthew d'Ancona of the Sunday Telegraph (who also edits The Spectator) all write exclusively political and Westminster-Village related columns. Only Simon Jenkins of the Guardian and the Sunday Times, George Monbiot of the Guardian and Richard Littlejohn of the Daily Mail, who write more generalised comment, came into the top ten columnists listed as being 'highly influential' in our poll findings.

It is slightly invidious to list a complete ranking of all the commentators, but suffice it to say that pretty much all of the main by-lined national newspaper commentators – as well as Anne McElvoy of the Evening

❞I don't want a chap in Whitehall or the White House changing his view because of what I write. I want to set people thinking – that's all❞ - Gideon Rachman

Leader columns:

The top ten pecking order of those whose influence in shaping government policy and government influence is 'huge':

1. The Daily Mail
2. The Sun
3. The Times
4. Mail on Sunday
5. Sunday Times
6. FT
7. Guardian
8. News of World
9. Telegraph
10. Sunday Telegraph

Blogs:

The blogs deemed most influential on British public policy and opinion:

1. Nick Robinson newslog (BBC)
2. Robert Peston (Pestons Picks - BBC)
3. Guido Fawkes
4. Comment is Free (The Guardian)
5. Comment Central (The Times)
6. Iain Dale's Diary joint 6th with Boulton & Co. (Sky News)
7. Red Box (The Times)
8. Roy Greenslade (The Guardian)
9. Ben Brogan (Daily Mail)
10. Brassneck (Daily Telegraph)

Standard which is a London – only paper garnered high results, either because of their visible prominence or because they write such pertinent and sought-after comment. Thus David Aaronovitch and Peter Riddell of the Times; Will Hutton of the Observer; Nick Cohen of the Observer and the Evening Standard; Jonathan Freedland of the Guardian; Daniel Finkelstein of the Times and Jeremy Clarkson of the Sunday Times all scored particularly highly.

Perhaps not surprisingly 71% said that they 'always' turn to the leader and comment pages. Slightly more people now read comment online (56%) but 68% say that blog comment is not as influential as print comment. As Catherine Meyer put it to us: "Whilst the print business model is no longer fit for purpose – the brand of key columnists remains strong, and of course comment attracts people to the web too."

It is hard to resist the suspicion that the time of the leader columns – especially in the upmarket press - has gone, and that they are kept on more for editorial vanity than from readers' demand. Certainly those we interviewed in person tended not to mention leaders. And yet respondents to our poll were robust in their enthusiasm for the influence of leaders.

> "comment is the essential intersection between the political classes and the public"
>
> – Charles Clarke MP

The Daily Grind:
What do commentators do?

(i) **They entertain.** Peter Oborne believes that he "tries to produce something that is agreeable to read on a weekly basis". Rachel Johnson notes that readability is a very large part of her concern. A number of the commentators, when asked to name their favourites, chose Matthew Parris of the Times, Lucy Kellaway of the FT, AA Gill of the Sunday Times and Boris Johnson of the Daily Telegraph (before he ended his column to run for Mayor) because of their ability to make their points, political or otherwise, with wit. Gill is included here because, though a restaurant and TV critic whose pieces do not appear on the op-ed pages, he nevertheless uses the form as polemic. In a Daily Mail piece on March 13 this year, headlined "Calm down dear, it's only my opinion!," Michael Winner, the restaurant critic and former film director, defended the right of his fine dining comrades – and all columnists – to be rudely funny. "What is to become of freedom of speech, common sense or national sanity if a critic – paid by a newspaper to criticise – cannot be critical?" It seems to work: Matthew Norman of the Independent, whose political comment is heavily spiced with wit, was named as Columnist of the Year in April's British Press Awards.

Denis MacShane, like Charles Clarke, mentioned the parliamentary sketch writers as serving a useful function in politics. They gave notice of new parliamentary talent (sometimes to those in a position to advance their political careers) and they attracted readers to learn about politics through humour. The late Hugo Young of The Guardian, among the most respected of columnists, wrote in an introduction to a collection of his columns published after his death in 2003 that, when he began in journalism in the 1950s, there was only one political column signed by its author. In the early 2000s, Young met an acquaintance who told him that he was compiling a list, for No 10, of all national newspaper columnists; he had reached 221, and was still counting.

> **"A huge number of ordinary people are saying we are voiceless, you write for us"**
> – Melanie Phillips

Editorial Intelligence now counts over 300 national newspaper columnists, summarising over 50,000 words of comment each day. That growth, in this most market-sensitive of industries, is driven by perceived demand. The demand comes from readers who want to be entertained. Martin Wolf of the FT marks a strong division between columns, like the majority of those on the FT, and the majority elsewhere. "What I try to do is write about what I think is important. It must make sense, and be clear. But clarity is complex, and it isn't often able to be summed up in a piece of polemical writing. I could not do that on a regular basis. I would feel untrue to the subject. But other columns do that, in the main. They confirm prejudices; they give a rush of adrenalin; they are fun. And in many cases, they are tremendously well written."

"I never feel powerful. I am writing for my mother. If I had one reader or half a million, I'd still write the same" – Anthony Hilton

When commentators are asked to name their favourites, or as Editorial Intelligence puts it, their 'Desert Island Columnists' they often name those whom they see as putting their views forcefully, even aggressively: Simon Jenkins of the Guardian and the Sunday Times, David Aaronovitch of the Times and Polly Toynbee of the Guardian stand out. Indeed, in a reflection of her position as the UK commentator with the most influence in our poll, Polly Toynbee appears to occupy a special place in the thoughts of her colleagues – even though they do not always agree with her views: Oborne qualified his praise for her by saying: "Polly is frightfully good. She is the manifestation of a polemical commentator, very partisan. There is a gorgeousness about a columnist who represents a political dogma: it's almost a form of integrity."

A new(ish) dimension to this is now obvious. Much contemporary comedy in the UK and elsewhere, especially the US, is built on the ridicule of politicians and to a lesser extent other public figures. That comedy includes: satirical shows on TV and radio; theatre and TV dramas which use undisguised or lightly disguised political figures who play more or less ridiculous or debased roles, usually based on "real" events; and the ability of some politicians – the Conservative London Mayoral candidate Boris Johnson, the Labour London Mayor Ken Livingstone and the former Liberal Democrat leader Charles Kennedy included - to make comedy from themselves and their colleagues on TV quiz shows and elsewhere. The success of these forms has made ridicule an accepted, though not always acceptable, part of the political scene in the UK. The stereotypes and characterisations of the political figures which are used in these comedies pass into "straight" political life and are used for political as well as comic effect. Currently, the image of a "dithering" Prime Minister Brown, originating in his change of mind, in the autumn of 2007, over calling an election, was greatly amplified not just by the commentariat but also by the comedy shows and is now inextricable from his image. The term "dithering,' was applied to the Prime Minister by commentators nearly sixty times between October 2007 and April 2008, accounting for one in every sixty mentions of him in total for everything he did or said. By late April the epithet was applied even more widely. Matthew d'Ancona wrote in the Sunday Telegraph: "It appears that this Government cannot even have a resignation crisis without dithering." This gave rise to what Tina Brown, writer, broadcaster and former Editor of Vanity Fair and the New Yorker describes as 'the view that enters the media bloodstream with great speed."

(ii) **They set agendas** and erect signposts for other journalists. All journalism runs on a series of meetings at which ideas for stories are put up, discussed, dismissed or pursued. Many of these are reportage of the main events of the day which the news outlet believes it should cover; others are the result of investigations by reporters; others will be analyses or features. All, however, especially the latter, work within a framework constructed, in part, by commentators who shape the way in which their fellows see the world. In a media universe as centralised in the London hothouse as is the British, the opinions of the big columnists are inevitably seen as the opinion formers of the opinion formers. Often named in this connection are FT commentators: Gideon Rachman on international affairs, Philip Stephens on UK and world politics and Martin Wolf on economic issues both in the UK and globally. Among newspapers, the FT, with the lowest circulation of any major daily in the UK, but with some half million global sales, commands a unique and sometimes unquestioned authority, both among (other) commentators and among the commentees. Also mentioned constantly for its quite different influence is the Daily Mail – often scorned, especially by the liberal commentators. It would see that as a badge of honour and Melanie Phillips, one of its most prominent commentators, stressed that was so – arguing that "there is no "right wing" press. The Daily Mail is widely seen as expressing, or provoking, the frustrations and demands of a large section of the middle class in a way that no other publication can match. On the other side of the barriers, Polly Toynbee enjoyed, last year, a moment of more than her customary fame when a leaked memo of an aide to Conservative leader David Cameron argued that the party must speak to those to whom her views appealed.

Alan Connor, a BBC journalist, says: "For sparking ideas and drawing attention to areas of interest, commentators are a great influence…in news planning meetings, and more informal chats in newsrooms, new concepts are more likely to be discussed if someone can refer to "that piece by John Naughton (who has a column in the Observer) or someone like that." A senior BBC radio 4 broadcast journalist who preferred to make his remarks off the record said that the commentariat "helps me frame questions and clarify issues for use on air. I would say this is a major influence on the way I do my job."

Mick Fealty, who began and runs the web log "Slugger O'Toole," an insider's take on the politics of Northern Ireland, and now writes "Brassneck," one of two Daily Telegraph bespoke political daily blogs, told us that "a Belfast news editor once told me that I was setting the agenda every day in Northern Ireland. Yes, the commentariat is powerful. Commentators can amplify what news journalists are reporting. So for instance, the Guardian correspondent in Belfast uncovered the real story of the McCartney pub murder of January 2005 (where a 33-year old man was stabbed to death in a murder widely attributed to the IRA) but blog commentators amplified the story even further than print news reporters and gave it greater impact."

Tina Brown said: "Columnists are very powerful because television is derivative of published opinion and picks it up and gives it staying power. When I went on TV I was always asked to express a view I had already written in my column."

(iii) **They say they tell the truth** and alert the people to the lies and falsehoods told to them, above all by politicians. This, speaking truth to power and to the people, is the single most common defining characteristic mentioned by columnist respondents: it is how they tend to see themselves. The job of the commentator, many say, is to reveal the truth behind the falsehood; or, less ambitiously, to cut through the welter of PR, news clips, debate, other commentary – and find the core of the issue.

This, surely, is an important task; yet the commentator most emphatic about his lack of power (and aversion to acquiring it) is also he who most emphatically claims to tell the truth. Peter Oborne said: "I try to tell the truth about what I see and what is happening in British political life. Public discourse has broadly become false discourse. The role of the commentator is to unpeel that and present the truth and explain it to the reader. There are hidden laws in politics just as there are in, say, physics. Our job is to explain how those laws work, bring them into the open".

Melanie Philips sees the job rather as Peter Oborne does: "I'm using my column to give voice to facts – in that way it becomes more difficult to dismiss. I'm always evidence-based…I set out to change the general public discourse by bringing to it something new, facts which are not usually presented. You must get the truth into public discourse…we shouldn't give up on objectivity…a culture will change only if it has the material to change, so you must put truths into the public domain". Many columnists use their columns as much to report as to opine. Columns carry the power they do because they are framed in a context which can best be described as emotional.

> **"Good print commentators influence the key opinion formers: shrill hucksters worry them."**
> – John Kelly, Publisher, Prospect

No other commentator was as definite as Oborne and Phillips – which may reflect to an extent the missionary quality the Daily Mail newspaper, under the editorship of Paul Dacre, can project. But others, more obliquely, assented: Mary Riddell's already quoted comment – that she only wrote pieces in which she "wholly believed" - matches Nick Cohen's belief that he brings the uncomfortable truth about radical Islam to the notice of politicians as well as to the Observer-reading public. Indeed, at least some columnists are said to attempt to gather and check their facts (not of course the same as arriving at the truth) as much as reporters do: the former minister Denis MacShane said he often read columnists to get facts as much as opinions since they did the shoe-leather or calling work more assiduously – Steve Richards of the Independent, Peter Riddell of the Times and Polly Toynbee of the Guardian were often mentioned in this regard by those we interviewed. Tina Brown, a Brit among Americans, said she often called as many as 20 contacts in the course of preparing one column.

"How to sum up impact? When the Sun and the Mail connects with the FT then you know you've got problems" – Mick Fealty, Brassneck and Slugger o'Toole

(iv) **They do battle.** Most columnists in an aggressive journalistic culture like the UK's seek, at least at times, to do battle. As we will see below, when they unite in a charge, or suddenly attack a figure or institution of whom they have previously written with general approval, the results are very noticeable. But a number of our interviewees singled out particular battles – in several cases, Martin Bright's revelations, in the New Statesman and on television (Channel Four's "Dispatches" programme), of the style and actions of London Mayor Ken Livingstone. Nick Cohen sees himself both as a revealer of ugly truths and as a battler against what he sees as the distortions of the left and of the beliefs of liberalism – "certainly there is a loose band of commentators and activists, in which I'd count myself, who are trying to shake liberalism out of its complacency – for instance on far right Islamism. Blogs like Normblog and Harry's Place feel like a political movement: this approach isn't for all columnists" (for a discussion of commentators and the worldwide web/blogs, see below).

Denis MacShane, Matthew Taylor and the un-named aide to a cabinet minister said they could not abide what MacShane called "the screechers" – those whose main weapon is outraged invective: he mentioned Richard Littlejohn and Melanie Philips of the Daily Mail and Jeremy Clarkson and Rod Liddle of the Sunday Times as examples. Matthew Taylor said of Simon Jenkins that while recognising his skill and literary ability, "[he] tire[d] of his approach, which is – "why is everyone so stupid? If I had power I would run things better." He's a sophisticated version of the Daily Mail". John Kelly, the publisher of Prospect remarked that it is the 'shrill hucksters' of the Commentariat who most worry those in power. He may well be right: Trevor Kavanagh of the Sun, whose sophistication is masked by such an approach in his column, is ranked in our poll one below Polly Toynbee for overall national influence on the comment scene.

(v) **They spot**, or set, trends. Many whom we interviewed thought this was the most important and useful function of columnists: Trevor Phillips, chairman of the Equality and Human Rights Commission, told us he thought this was the only source of the commentariat's power. The social commentator, columnist and businessman Peter York says: "The kind of journalism which reveals a social movement, and which describes and writes about it well, can change people's perception of a culture and thus can, I think, change behaviour. I think of Tom Wolfe (the US journalist and novelist, who wrote on the sixties hippy culture, seventies radical culture and – in his novels – the morals and actions of US business) in this regard: he changed the sensibility of young educated people, as to the way they thought about culture". Howell James sees the skill of commentators – and of editors – in spotting and riding trends just a little ahead of the mass of people – a view shared by Christopher Meyer at the PCC: both mentioned the Sun, especially in the eighties, in this context.

Howell James said "Why, now, would thoughtful people move to Barrack Obama – or in the nineties, to Tony Blair or Margaret Thatcher in the seventies and eighties? The commentators set much of this trend, through a subtle reading of the popular mood. That forced people to review their perspectives. Though I do think The Sun has found post-Thatcher life difficult." When talking to us about tuition fees (see above), the former minister Charles Clarke said that commentators "give intellectual

> **"There is a star system which has filtered through to newspapers..there is a relationship between star columnists and their editors and the reason is because of their power with the public**. – Michael Green

underpinning and create intellectual fashion". The public relations consultant Omerli Cohen makes an allied but slightly different point, saying that columns can herald counter-trends, allowing new thoughts to be voiced even to oneself – "the commentariat influences me in that it gives me a vocabulary, or justification, to voice my views and also gives me insight into how the world considers an issue. It also helps justify 'outlaw' opinions, when I feel embarrassed that, yet again, I feel uncomfortable with received opinion on a topic."

(vi) **They form, or speak to, constituencies**. A number of those whom we interviewed made a distinction – often a sharp one – between speaking to power and speaking to the people. Suzanne Moore of the Mail on Sunday said: "I am writing much more for the readers and much less for my peers than when I was at The Guardian or the Independent. That is one of the main differences between a broadsheet and a tabloid-style column, I feel. You have to take much less for granted in the middle or tabloid market –

including, I would say, political views".

One constituency, for many the most valued, is the establishment. Richard Lambert, a former editor of the FT and now director general of the Confederation of British Industries, speaks of the role of commentators as adding value to a busy life, saying: "I am strongly in favour of the heavily researched kind of columns, columns which speak from some insight gathered. For example, a piece written by Philip Stephens (chief political commentator of the FT) after he had seen Tony Blair is going to be very useful. But the why-oh-why pieces are a waste of time. I want to know what's going on: or to be introduced to new ideas. So I never miss the Economist (another interviewee described the Economist as "one long magnificent opinionated column.")

Within that split, between speaking truth (or opinion) to power and telling it to the people, there are many other divisions. Some commentators – Polly Toynbee at The Guardian, Simon Heffer and Janet Daley of the Daily Telegraph, David Aaronovitch of the Times and Martin Kettle of the Guardian were mentioned by our interviewees several times – are seen as speaking to or even helping to create particular constituencies. Interestingly, Nick Cohen dissents from many of his colleagues in not seeing the act of speaking truth to power as one of always criticising those who hold power implicitly or explicitly in the act of doing so – "I don't see myself as having anything in common with some idiot on the Independent. I have far more in common with, say, David Miliband. I don't accept the absolute division between journalists and politicians." It is a point which David Aaronovich often makes in his Times columns.

Those who write for the elite do often think the effort worth-while. Apart from the many instances of anecdotal evidence that shafts were hitting home, two commentators mentioned that their target audience had permanently open minds. Tina Brown, quoting the electoral strategist Mark Penn (who resigned from Hilary Clinton's campaign while this report was being completed) said that she believed that columns appealed to "an impressionable elite." Peter York took the thought further, saying: "Educated middle-class people are fantastically impressionable. I believe I could change the minds of most of them with a column, or a dinner party conversation."

(vii) **They change their minds.** A public change of mind is a very powerful weapon for a high profile columnist, though not one that can be used too often. While we were interviewing for this report, The Times' economic commentator, Anatole Kaletsky, began a column (January 22, 2008) with - "There can be no more doubt. Northern Rock is Gordon Brown's Black Wednesday. The Prime Minister, like John Major before him, remains in office, but he is no longer in power." This was, said the Telegraph Media Group's columnist Iain Martin, a major talking point for days in the circles in which he moved – because Kaletsky had been seen to be largely supportive of Brown's economic policy when Chancellor.

Matthew Taylor said: "Particularly influential can be those commentators who take a reliable line and then change their minds. For example, it would have an impact if Philip Stephens (the FT commentator, strongly in favour of a more integrated Europe) called for a referendum on the EU treaty. Also, if moderate columnists get outraged then you look at it – a piece from a balanced commentator who says: this is unconscionable – you would certainly look at." Denis MacShane gave the example of George Monbiot (a Guardian columnist who took a strongly anti-nuclear line), who wrote a column saying he had been convinced that the UK needed nuclear power stations for ecological reasons – and of the Oxford scholar and Guardian columnist Timothy Garton Ash, who is also strongly supportive of the European Union, calling for a referendum – adding, pointedly – "I thought he was on our side!" Influence, said Howell James, "comes either from the constant drip drip of a powerful commentator, or when columnists decides to change their mind, when that happens ministers and officials take notice."

(viii) **They have the power** to destroy ministerial and other public careers, or at least substantially affect reputations. This power has been with journalism for at least a century and a half: the reporting and commentary from Crimea of The Times' William Howard Russell, highlighting poor military strategy and wretched conditions for the soldiers – aided by the new telegraph - was at least influential in forcing the resignation of the government of the Earl of Aberdeen in 1855. Journalism's period of greatest power was ushered in by the reporting of Bob Woodward and Carl Bernstein for the Washington Post, which helped cause the resignation of President Richard Nixon in 1974. Many in the news media see their finest hours as being those in which cabinet ministers resigned after a press campaign as have, in the Blair governments, Peter Mandelson (twice), David Blunkett (twice) and Stephen Byers. In all cases (including the Earl of Aberdeen's) the facts have been the determining feature, but the commentariat, as many of its members say, amplify the reporting and give judgment on whether or not the issue is a resigning matter.

Some commentators believe that forcing a resignation is now more difficult than it was. Iain Martin said: "Blair came into office determined that what happened to Major would not happen to him. He believed that if you ignored scandals they would, in the main, go away. Blair has re-written the rules in this: and the problem for the commentariat is: What do you do when everything does go away? Look at (Metropolitan Police Commissioner) Ian Blair – essentially he said: go ahead, fire me. And you can get a perverse reaction: when everyone was calling for the resignation of (Archbishop) Rowan Williams, the synod gave him an ovation. Even if you are tarnished – and those round Blair believed that everyone in public life was tarnished in some way – you weather it."

The "political theatre of the sketch writers," as Charles Clarke described it – these are columnists whose identity is somewhere between a diarist, a

"when columnists decide to change their mind, ministers and officials take notice" - Howell James

political reporter and an op-ed writer - can, itself, be potent and trigger more comment elsewhere in the newspapers. In March this year, daily parliamentary sketch writers picked up Ed Balls, the Education Secretary, as apparently saying "So what?" in response to a Conservative charge that the tax burden was high. He maintained – and the Hansard report showed – that he had said: "So weak!" Commentators insinuated that he had caused the Hansard record to be amended. Hostile comment about Balls gathered pace, fuelled by his assertion in April that faith schools were contravening government policy on charging for access. Nearly fifty comment pieces were published about him over just eight weeks, prompting two leaders from the Daily Mail in the space of four days, one of which asked whether he had become Labour's biggest electoral liability. The Conservative Shadow Children's Secretary Michael Gove MP (himself a columnist for the Times) claimed in mid-April that the Secretary of State had made concessions which 'were not a total retreat, but definitely a climb-down.'

We were reminded, in doing this report, of the alleged dictum of Alastair Campbell, Tony Blair's director of strategy and communications, that a minister under pressure could not survive 13 days on the front page. Howell James said that there was no such precision – but that "if you are being battered constantly in the columns it can be hard to resist calls for a departure. The media don't cause the problem but they have a strong impact on the nature of the crisis. Everything is defined by the ability to spot the tipping point – when defence runs out."

....

Hug Your Enemy Very Close:
Managing the Commentariat

Those in power manage the commentariat in a variety of ways according to the nature of the commentator. Matthew Taylor told us that, in the Blair No10, commentators were split into four types – one of which, the mind-changers, we've already noted (above).

"The other three were "the drip-drip ones – columns of a particular bent, who will just keep having a go at you. Janet Daley on the right at the Daily telegraph and Kevin Maguire (of the Daily Mirror) on the left are examples of that. A press officer's job was to try to moderate them – but it was a desperate exercise. Then there are the people who grab an issue and put it on the agenda and who can get it across in a dramatic way. They can often point to something interesting, and they often want briefings and real information. Polly Toynbee is the best example of that. And there are the "Westminster only" people – Andrew Rawnsley (of the Observer), Fraser Nelson (of the Spectator and the News of the World) and Peter Riddell (of the Times). They can have a real impact, depending on what they reveal more than anything else: Andrew Rawnsley's book on Blair-Brown was full of revelations. Others can be quite valuable but clearly bear one set of fingerprints: we all assumed Robert Peston's biography of Gordon (Brown) came largely from Ed Balls: and many of Jackie Ashley's columns (in the Guardian) seemed to be from the same general area. There's nothing much you can do about that."

The professionals within the Westminster circle agreed that the jagged edges of the commentators could be greatly smoothed by an invitation to No. 10 or the Treasury - or, even better, to Chequers. Charlie Whelan, the former Brown aide, was typically cynical. "We'd call in X and have a nice cup of tea so they'd be nice about Gordon for a few months. They love it at Chequers or Downing Street." Denis MacShane makes the same point, as does Christopher Meyer. Blair, more than Brown, was an inveterate bender of the ears of the commentariat, especially in his early years, and especially of those whom he expected to disagree with him. Some of those to whom we spoke thought this worked well at first, but less well when doubts began to form

> **"Commentator's Independence gives them power...a daisy chain of bad columns are feared more than a bad opinion poll"**
> – Denis MacShane MP

– and badly in his later years, especially after the Iraq war. And those who arranged these chats do not always respect those who come in: a senior ministerial aide said: "When a commentator has clearly been in for a chat at No.10 and comes out to write a distinctly friendly piece it may be welcome but it's lazy journalism."

The commentators react to being "managed" in different ways – usually, by stressing distance. Peter Oborne said that "certain commentators value access and become instruments of a faction. Many of my colleagues are not commentators at all, but manifestations of a fundamentally debased system. The absence of any personal contact with their subject matter is the nirvana to which all commentators should aspire, especially as we grow older. Private contact is corrupting."

Melanie Phillips says that she does seek and agrees to briefings – "you must see people because after a while it becomes obvious you have no facts" and admits: "It's always the case that when you speak to people your position becomes more nuanced, because the issue comes to seem more complex – though sometimes you become more definite in your view from speaking to

There are two different kinds of columnist. First, there's the insider,who co-operates with politicians and floats ideas which ministers or shadow ministers want floated. Then there's the outsider, who largely scorns professional politicians. He may be able to change the political climate, very slowly, by saying what is originally unsayable, and making it thinkable. – Peter Hitchens

people: it isn't all one way." Mary Riddell said that relationships between political writers and politicians "should be close enough to be trusted as someone who is deemed fair and to have inside information." David Seymour, the former political editor of Mirror Group Newspapers, said that the two sides "should not be close, but should have a relationship so that each side understands the other." All these responses assume there to be a fundamental difference of interest between commentariat and politicians. In distinction, Nick Cohen presents a radical challenge to this, seeing politicians not as from a different species but as people with whose ideas he might or might not agree – as he regards fellow commentators.

Rising Tide of Opinion:
Broadcast v Print v Blogs

If there are now some 300 columnists in the UK, there are now some 100 million blogs worldwide – and thus the columnist must try harder than ever to be noticed.

Most agree that the judicious posing of the problem, with problems on both sides, no longer cuts it except in rare and authoritative cases – Peter Riddell of the Times and Steve Richards of the Independent are most often mentioned here. Many commentators place stress on, or value others', good writing. Nick Cohen says: "I worry whether I have written an ugly sentence, I'd be far more horrified by a grammatical error than anything else." Several people commended Simon Jenkins for a style which mixes the elegant and the acerbic. As Stefan Stern of the FT, put it: "Does it change anybody's behaviour - who can tell? I hope it has at least some influence; otherwise, as Basil Fawlty might say, "What's the bleedin' point?!"

The distaste for "screechers" is a common reaction by the insiders, especially those on the left for those on the right. Many columnists, however, see "screeching" as robust polemic. Rachel Johnson of the Sunday Times, whose columns mix social comment with personal experience, said: "There's a lot of pressure to be noticed, more and more. My first thought when I write is always – how do I make this readable? My second is: what will I end up saying? I think, now, you always have to ramp up your reaction, to give the readers something meaty to chew on. During the Heather Mills-Paul McCartney divorce case, I thought about writing something nice about her, but the Sunday Times steered me to dislike her. There are different rules for different columnists though, and Jeremy Clarkson (the motoring writer who has a general column in the Sunday Times) gets away with most. You've got everyone doing the high-voltage thing: there's a real ramping up industry here. That said, the US press is desperately in need of some British-type stuff. It's quite pallid. The British palate has got used to spice." Timothy Garton Ash of the Guardian says: "I think it is true that the pressure is to shout louder and louder: and that must be resisted. But you cannot write simply on the one hand and on the other. There must be clarity."

As we've noted above, commentators often report, and, according to at least Melanie Phillips, reporters often comment: "newspapers should be the conduit of fact, but you can't rely on that any longer because reporters have become so opinionated." Catherine Meyer agrees, saying that the "division between comment and reporting has become steadily eroded, so it's difficult to know where comment ends and reporting begins." Both reporters and commentators are borrowing from each other to make a bigger splash, a search all the more urgent because of the blogosphere (see below). Insiders agree, and deplore: in a 2005 speech, Howell James said: "The problem (of communication) is compounded because we are dependent to some degree on messages communicated via the media, who, like markets, always tend to overshoot. And you can see why: a major risk will always be a better story than a modest one."

Television has long been seen by newspaper journalists with some suspicion: but most are now reconciled to the fact that, for the large majority of the population of the UK (as elsewhere), TV is the dominant means of information – and, as MacShane says: "Most people get their opinions from television." However, as the BBC's Alan Connor noted, TV journalists depend to a very large degree on stories and opinions in newspapers for the agenda they construct and the attitudes they adopt. The US-based Tina Brown describes how an agenda is shaped: "It's a loop, it's the movement of a story from YouTube to cable news video loop plus the comment axis… cable news only looks for a sound bite, and gets a "gotcha" moment... "The View" then passes from cable to the network morning news shows and thence into print, which in the US plays catch-up – and that's where it gets another set of legs, a week of discussion in print." Though the British and other versions of the loop will be different, the principle is the same – commentary gets into broadcast news and current affairs programmes, is then amplified, sets the news agenda, and then ricochets out again for more print comment.

The Internet is changing everything – though no-one is quite sure yet how. On one level, it means that most print can be read anywhere in the world – with a built-in advantage for the Anglophone press, because of the increasing spread of English as a second language. Denis MacShane recalled with pleasure how he had been called "Macshame" in a Sun headline – to be greeted later that same day, in Germany by the then German Foreign Minister, Joschka Fischer, with a "Guten Tag, Herr Macshame!" Many of those to whom we spoke mentioned non-British-based columnists as Andrew Sullivan, Christopher Hitchens, Matt Drudge or Joe Klein – as favoured reads.

However, for the commentators especially (more, it seems, than for most insiders on our evidence), the net and blogs are beginning to make a substantial difference. Many of them read blogs – some, like Nick Cohen's reading of Harry's Place and Normblog, to check similar opinions to their own, others, like Alan Connor of the BBC, to discover strange views through an astonishing range of sites, comprising BBC Internet Blog, Potlatch by Will Davies, Oblomovka, Phil Gyford, Tomski, Adam Smith Institute, Beau Beau d'Or, Ben Brogan, Biased BBC, Martin Bright, Channel4FactCheck, OrderOrder, Make My Vote Count, My Right Wing Dad, Open Democracy, Richard Allan, Samizdata, Nick Robinson, Evan Davies, Mark Mardell, Robert Peston, Roy Greenslade, Martin Moore, Adrian Monck, City of Sound, Currybet, James Cridland, Story Curve, Bill Thompson, EMC Media Blog, Broken TV, Watching TV Online, Lost Remote, Steven Berlin Johnson and Audiotheque – an eclectic mixture of political, media, informed and opinionated comment – all free. A prominent Radio 4 presenter told us that "my impression is that, at Westminster, some key bloggers (Iain Dale, Ben Brogan, Nick Robinson) are now being used to get information out in real time in a way that traditional media couldn't do. This was noticeable in the cases of (former cabinet minister) Peter Hain and (Scottish Labour Party leader) Wendy Alexander, when rumours and developments were flagged up by bloggers long before news bulletins." Both were embroiled in allegations of financial impropriety: Hain resigned in January 2008; Alexander was found by the Electoral Commission to have taken significant steps to comply with the funding regulations,' and was not referred to the procurator fiscal.

Mick Fealty, the professional blogger, says that bloggers are now, with commentators, contributing to what he calls "the grand narrative" – though he admits that "measuring the impact of blogs on the mainstream media is a real problem because journalists never acknowledge their source even when it is another media source. They don't give credit where it is due – which, these days, is often to blogs, not newspapers." Catherine Meyer of Time believes that "clearly the influence of print is declining and that of the blogosphere is increasingly important. So while newspapers are declining – the print business model is no longer fit for purpose – the brand of key columnists remains strong, and comment attracts people to the web."

In the past two years, newspaper blogs, mainly or wholly about politics, have increased their reach and their importance, The Guardian has Comment is Free; the Times, Red Box; the Telegraph has Brassneck and Three Line Whip. A recent start-up, wholly devoted to political issues, is

PoliticsHome, the brain child of Stefan Shakespeare of the polling company YouGov Martin Bright of the New Statesman and Tim Montgomerie of ConservativeHome, another influential blog. Andrew Rawnsley, The Observer's anchor Sunday commentator deems political comment on the web sufficiently interesting to have become the editor in chief of PoliticsHome, writing a daily comment piece which summarises the thoughts of the 'PH100' influencers asked to comment in a daily online poll.

Those columnists who are also bloggers are enthusiastic about the new medium. One of the most popular is Melanie Philips: "Blogging has taken over my life. I started after the second intifada (in 2000). I do one to six posts a day. I am a fact-based columnist because I am a facts-based person. I strive for objectivity. You can no longer rely on news as the sole basis of fact. Blogging democratises because it breaks the grip of the dominant narrative and exposes it to huge criticism… being read, and responded to, is influence." Iain Martin said he was initially suspicious: "I did think that it would dilute mine and others' writing, we would have nothing left to say" – but says that he is now an enthusiast: "I found it was a virtuous circle – the blogging fed into the column, the column into the blog. And it is a quite different style of comment, which will become increasingly important. You link to and collaborate with colleagues elsewhere. In the column world you would never write a column on Gordon Brown which gave references for other pieces on the same issue: it was part of our vanity. But blogging isn't like that; you are part of a network, not a lone wolf."

The enthusiasm shown by some in the commentariat for blogging is not universally shared. A column by Jonathan Freedland in the Guardian, much discussed, pointed to the abusive and extreme nature of much blog comment – including on his own newspaper's blog, Comment is Free. Ian Wylie of the autism charity TreeHouse Trust says: "There is a very clear difference between bloggers and newspaper comment: the latter has a reputation to preserve. There is a level of critical scrutiny and editorial judgment in newspaper by-lined comment that is completely absent from blogs, making them little more than online pub chatter – entertaining, sometimes hitting their target, but too often unreliable."

The emphasis on personality and on features which can fit into magazine or TV chat show formats – as against "serious" political and analytical commentary – is now given extra force by the new political scandal websites. Since his revelation of the affair between President Bill Clinton and Monica Lewinsky, Matt Drudge has built a hobby for discovering and retailing scandal into a powerful media operation, one which now has real leverage over, for example, the current presidential campaign in the US. Nothing in the UK approaches his influence, though the conservative-inclined websites Iain Dale's Diary and Guido Fawkes's Order-Order.com – especially the latter – have used the same techniques. Fawkes originated news of an affair between former Labour Deputy Leader John Prescott and his diary secretary; he posted an allegation of a "love child" whose parents were said to be two well-known political commentators (the story was injuncted before it could appear elsewhere); and at the time of writing is promising a revelation of a further scandal concerning an MP's daughter – "If you are the daughter of an MP, living in Kentish Town, shacked up with a druggie barrister inclined to having loud all-night parties. Turn the noise down, your neighbour is threatening to shop you."

Lines here are hard to draw. Politicians increasingly use personal and family details in their self presentation. Tony and Cherie Blair famously boasted of a hyperactive sex life to the Sun before the 2005 general election. The editorial policies – and success – of celebrity magazines like Hello and the show business editors of newspapers and TV shows are built on carefully calibrated relationships between the journalists and the publicists. These techniques are now spreading, inexorably, to politicians, especially to party leaders constantly in the public eye, constantly appraised on personal, familial and moral grounds by a commentariat which itself, as a body, is reluctant to draw lines between private and public actions and morality.

Noting the capacity for the web to involve the users as well as the writers, Howell James said: "I think we're in transition – between influencing the public and the public finding things out for themselves on the web. I don't think the commentators have lost their potency yet: but the web is changing and will change them."

"When you write or say something it plays to different people at different levels and then suddenly the discourse changes" – Melanie Phillips

of the Daily Mail and online on www.spectator.co.uk

We began by highlighting the modesty of many of those interviewed respondents from the Commentariat in the matter of their power. Yet it seems clear that, whether or not they sincerely believe that they have little or no influence, that belief is false. Commentators are taken seriously by most of those who constitute the political class: and, in one way or another, they take themselves seriously too. If their trade is on the brink of change, it remains in robust form now: and may find that the world wide web, while ushering in a vast multiplicity of voices, may be as kind to them as print has come to be.

Editorial Intelligence case studies

Number Crunching

In order to look at the impact of the commentariat Editorial Intelligence's Sophie Radice took four very different issues affecting public policy and public opinion and analysed the stance and number of comment pieces across a broad spectrum of newspapers to set them in context of political decisions which were taken at the time. The subjects chosen were the finance trio of The Northern Rock, non-doms and capital gains tax issues (which were also analysed separately), Heathrow and the plans for a third runway, supercasinos and finally, the treatment of the Gurkhas.

For the Northern Rock crisis we looked at the huge wave of commentary in the six months leading up to nationalisation and considered if the opinions of commentators had any influence on government U-turns and changes of heart. In our analysis we grouped it with tax issues of non-domiciled residents (non-doms) and capital gains because these three subjects were so often grouped together by the commentators.

For the subject of Heathrow's runway expansion we looked at the same six month period from October 2007 to March 2008 and produced a graph depicting which papers were for or against the idea of a third runway. It became clear that the number of comment pieces on a subject was not necessarily indicative of who was the most vigorous opponent of the idea because even though the Daily Express wrote the greatest number of commentary pieces coming out against the Heathrow expansion, the Sunday Times comment pieces were the most sharply critical and negative in tone.

For the supercasinos the analysed time period was extended and changed (January 2007- to January 2008) because of Gordon Brown's decision to scrap the supercasinos which came when he took over as Prime Minister in June 2007 and the commentary had been a steady and usually disapproving trickle rather then a single mass. It was therefore more useful in this case to look at a whole year, rather then an intense six-month period. For the Gurkhas too, it was more informative to cover a ten-month period, running from June 2007, to the end of March 2008, so that we could look at how the subject had gradually gained momentum.

Between a rock and a hard place

The Northern Rock crisis was the subject most keenly covered by commentators and leaders of the national papers in the six months from October 2007 to March 2008.

With 763 comment pieces on the stricken bank, it surpassed commentary on Iraq by 300 columns and Barack Obama by nearly 600. The collapse of the Newcastle based mortgage provider was a drawn-out British saga, with greedy bosses, shady private equity firms (JC Flowers, Cerberus and Blackstone) the home-grown hero (Richard Branson) and the oppressed down-trodden share holders and tax payers. There was such a large cast of people, institutions and decisions to point the finger at – the FSA, the Northern Rock directors, the Bank of England, the Treasury, Gordon Brown's 1997 financial changes and of course the indecisive foot-dragging of a seemingly bewildered government, which many commentators agreed should have acted earlier.

Understandably financial commentators couldn't really bring themselves to write about much else. It wasn't just the financial journalists either, Richard Littlejohn in the Daily Mail on February 19 blamed the 'spivs' at Northern Rock for 'knocking out monster mortgages to minimum-wage monkeys'[1] while Rod Liddle in The Sunday Times (November 18) wrote that Northern Rock was 'portrayed as an act of God, like a freak flood. But, of course, it is not: it has been occasioned by the greed and stupidity of men like Applegarth'.[2]

Although Northern Rock dominated the column inches it led a platoon of capital gains tax and non-doms tax change issues. Here was the new government looking so dithery that few commentators could resist throwing a punch or three. The constant analysis of this embarrassing trio of topics, often mentioned in the same breath, helped create a climate of U-turns and changes of heart from the government which in turn seemed to do little to quiet criticism from the commentariat.

Subjects most commented on between October 2007 and March 2008

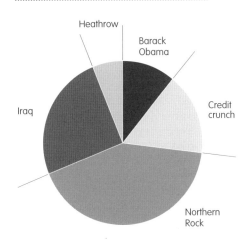

[1] Richard Littlejohn, The Daily Mail, 19th February 2008. [2] Rod Liddle, The Sunday Times, 18th November 2007

Between a rock and a hard place:

Capital gains tax and non-doms

Pre-budget proposals on changes to capital gains tax changes and non-doms' tax were understood by commentators to have been put forward as popularist moves to show that the government was doing something about division between the super wealthy and the very poor of Britain – a subject that many columnists wrote about during 2007.

Although the non-dom tax plans were seen as directly lifted from the Conservative Party conference both tax changes were meant to hit the private equity fat cats by plugging up tax loopholes and some columnists and leaders at least appreciated the sentiment. Before the pre-budget report of October 9 The Financial Times leader (October 2) urged Labour to do something to tackle the 'bizarre anomaly by which international billionaires can keep their money offshore, live in London and not pay a penny in tax'.[3] The Daily Mail, October 23, Alex Brummer defended the pre-budget report's handling of the non-doms and capital-gains tax by saying that business lobbies cannot 'have it both ways', by asking for tax simplification and less red tape on one hand and on the other asking for special exemptions for entrepreneurship. Who added that, 'the real key for enterprise is access to start up capital, not the tax bill when assets are cashed out'.[4]

By the time the actual budget came around on March 12 the national mood had changed. Small businesses had petitioned the government because they felt they were going to be penalised and the wealthy non-doms were supposedly threatening to move away from London. Most commentators felt that Alistair Darling had accidentally lashed out at the wrong people and that small businesses in particular were right to be angry. Darling had already promised a revision of capital gains tax by offering relief to small businesses relief in November while February saw a get out clause for non-doms when the chancellor said that he would no longer require them to make additional disclosures about their income and gains arising abroad. Commentators such as The Evening Standard's Chris Blackhurst who had seemed keen on Darling doing something about non-doms in the Autumn felt by the following February that it could do Britain's reputation as a financial haven a great deal of harm.[5] The over-whelming commentariat view by March (excluding the Guardian's Nils Pratley and Polly Toynbee who were consistently unsympathetic to the view that the financial services would really be damaged by these taxes [6]) was that climate had changed dramatically in the last six months and that the tax plans were thought up on the hoof.

A day after the 2008 budget in which the chancellor protected small businesses

[3] Leader, The Financial Times, 2nd October 2007. [4] Alex Brummer, The Daily Mail, 23rd October 2007. [5] Chris Blackhurst, The Evening Standard, 25th February 2008. [6] Nils Pratley, The Guardian, 13th March, Polly Toynbee, The Guardian 29th February 2008. Copyright Editorial Intelligence Ltd 2008. Do not reproduce without permission.

and created loop-holes for non-doms, Adrian Hamilton in the Independent (March 13) summed up the national mood, now more anxious about recession than hitting the wealthy and deeply shaken by what had happened to Northern Rock. Hamilton said that when it came to taxes, politicians tend to react to last year's mood just as circumstances are changing and that now that the 'City is engulfed in the biggest financial crisis for a generation, or even the war' it may well be 'the wrong fight, at the wrong time, in the wrong place.' [7]

....

Between a rock and a hard place:
Northern Rock

After the drama of the late summer of 2007 with the Bank of England giving Northern Rock emergency funds on September 28, October saw 113 comments by the commentariat picking over what to do, who was to blame and what lessons should be learnt.

Each week seemed to bring a new potential buyer for the bank and while some commentators felt that Richard Branson was simply courting publicity, others, such as Lucy Farndon, writing in the Daily Mail on October 13 saw him as an 'unlikely saviour'[8] whose intervention should be welcomed by shareholders because they would be able to enjoy the benefits if he turned the business around. In October too, Alistair Darling failed to impress commentators when he

appeared in front of the Treasury Select Committee and many writers looked back to financial systems devised by Gordon Brown and Ed Balls in 1997. In the Daily Telegraph of October 22 Liam Halligan asked for a reversal of some of this financial legislation which took responsibility for banking supervision away from Threadneedle Street and gave it to the Financial Services Authority, leaving the bank in charge of financial stability yet reliant on the FSA for information.[9]

November saw outrage from all quarters of the commentariat as bidders for Northern Rock urged the Bank of England to waive interest charges of £2bn on its crisis loan and many wondered how the tax payer would be expected to foot such a massive bill. Nationalisation became a very real possibility with the Daily Mail leader on November 15 asking how many more millions of taxpayers would have to stump up if the bank fell under the dead hand of the state.[10] By the 20th the Daily Mail had thought up the radical idea of making the financial community foot the bill for its own problems ' then the rest of us might be less resentful of those vast City bonuses'.[11] This was the month when commentators became really excited with many of them arguing over the benefits or evils of a nationalised bank – there were nearly 200 columns on the subject.

December saw Northern Rock's chief executive resign, something nearly all financial commentators throughout the British media had been asking for, and in the Guardian, both its leader and its writer Nils Pratley agreed on December 14 that nationalisation was really the only option.[12] The Daily Express's Andrew

[7] Adrian Hamilton, The Independent,13th March 2008. [8] Lucy Farndon, The Daily Mail 13th October 2007. [9] Liam Halligan, The Daily Telegraph, 22nd October 2007. [10] Leader, The Daily Mail, 15th November 2007. [11] Leader, The, Daily Mail, 20th November 2007. [12] Nils Pratley, The Guardian, 14th December 2007. Copyright Editorial Intelligence Ltd 2008. Do not reproduce without permission.

Johnson writing on January 15 felt that nationalisation would be a nightmare for the Government, battering its reputation for financial management and raising the spectre of the Treasury repossessing homes from the defaulting Rock. On February 17 Alistair Darling announced that the two proposals tabled for Northern Rock, one from a group led by Virgin and the other from in-house management- wouldn't actually offer enough value to the taxpayer and that the Rock would have to be nationalised. 109 comment pieces were written about the nationalisation of Northern Rock in the last two weeks of February. Of these perhaps one of the most thought-provoking was by

Peter Oborne in the Daily Mail on February 23 who said he had learnt that Goldman Sachs advised the government that some form of public ownership for Northern Rock was the only sensible solution all the way back in September. Oborne wanted to know why the government had spent so much time and public money trying to avoid the nationalisation of Northern Rock that was possibly inevitable from the beginning. He asked for the debate to be kept alive and for real answers from the government about what happened [13]. On March 19 Northern Rock said that it would have to cut 2,000 jobs and reduce its residential mortgage lending by half.

Number of comments pieces on non-doms, capital gains tax changes and Northern Rock Oct 2007- March 2008

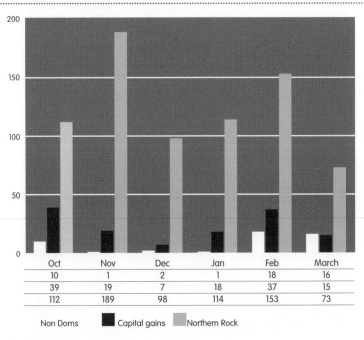

	Oct	Nov	Dec	Jan	Feb	March
Non Doms	10	1	2	1	18	16
Capital gains	39	19	7	18	37	15
Northern Rock	112	189	98	114	153	73

[13] Peter Oborne, The Daily Mail, 23rd February 2008. Copyright Editorial Intelligence Ltd 2008. Do not reproduce without permission.

Heathrow

The case for a third runway at Heathrow was discussed by 112 commentators in the six month period from October 2007 to March 2008.

This discussion included their opinions on the hands-off attitude of Ferrovial (the Spanish owner of the British Airports Authority) the case against expansionism, a more plausible site for a new airport in the East End of London, the crash landing of a passenger plane on January 17, protesters on the House of Commons' roof, the BAA's agreement with the Civil Aviation Authority about raising landing charges and the security breach just before the Queen's visit on March 13.

Those who felt that a new terminal was inevitable and necessary such as the writers of the Evening Standard leaders throughout the six months period analysed had considerable reservations The Evening Standard invited Zac Goldsmith to write a guest column hoping that 'just this once the Government prioritises the quality of London life above the short term interests of the aviation industry'[14] on November 12. The Evening Standard clearly stated that it favoured another runway, but that the Government should take a much more robust approach to the aviation industry than it does at present. All writers, even those in favour of the new runway, wrote negatively about the existing experience of being a passenger at Heathrow, of the bad service, long security queues, and 'squalor' of the surroundings. Financial writers told stories of businessmen who

choose not to fly to London because they couldn't face going through the airport.

The Sun Leader of February 28 came out strongly against the runway, saying that the environmental costs would be too great [15]. Simon Jenkins in the Sunday Times of November 25 wrote that denying approval for a third runway would have actually boosted the economy by encouraging more people to holiday at home and helped fight global warming. He ended with the terse statement– 'all we do know is that the government's case for a third Heathrow runway is so thin as to amount to a single sentence. BA wants it.'[16]

On January 31 2008 Camilla Cavendish of The Times stated that she felt that the British public was being conned over the need for a new runway. Cavendish did not believe that the airport was full or that there was any important economic reason for doing it as she very much doubted that aviation has such a huge impact on the economy. Similarly she felt that arguments over the environment, capacity and usage didn't hold water.' At one stroke we are looking at a con, perhaps the greatest ever perpetrated on the British people by the DTI'. Such a distortion she felt, suggested that the DTI had ceased to function as an arm of the government and had become a mere

[14] Zac Goldsmith, The Evening Standard, 12th November 2007. [15] Leader, The Sun, 28th February 2008. [16] Simon Jenkins, The Sunday Times, "5th November 2007. [17] Camillla Cavendish, The Times, 31st January 2008. Copyright Editorial Intelligence Ltd 2008. Do not reproduce without permission.

subsidiary of BAA [17].

The Sunday Times leader of March 9 went even further when writing about the government document putting the case forward for a third runway which was published on the same day. The Sunday Times felt that 'data on the impact of a third runway was repeatedly altered' and suspected that it was due to collusion with BAA. The Sunday Times concluded that, 'Ministers seem so beholden to BAA and Heathrow that they have closed their minds to the alternatives, whatever the cost to the environment and the quality of life.'[18]

The debacle of the Heathrow's fifth terminal opening on March 27, had 22 columns written about it in the last days of March with only one – the Daily Telegraph leader of the 28th - showing some optimism that 'teething problems would be overcome'[19]. The Daily Mail, Daily Express and the Financial Times leaders wanted BA's chief executive Willie Walsh to resign and were depressed about the whole future of the airport, while The Guardian saw the terminal's messy opening as a clear reason to rethink any other kind of air-port expansion. The Sunday Times, the harshest critic of plans for a new terminal throughout the six months analysed, saw Terminal 5 as symptomatic of underlying problems with the airport itself and that ' the lesson of Terminal 5 chaos is that however much you spend trying to bring Heathrow into the 21st century, its fundamental problems will remain'.[20]

Number of comment pieces on Heathrow Oct 2007- March 2008

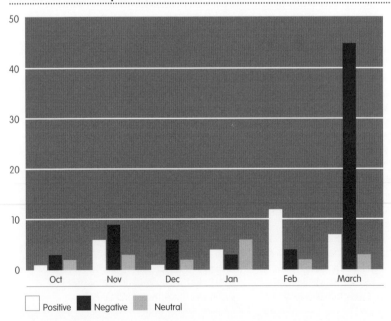

18 Leader, The Sunday Times, 9th March 2008. 19 Leader, The Daily Telegraph, 28th March 2008. 20 Leader, The Sunday Times, 30th March 2008. Copyright Editorial Intelligence Ltd 2008. Do not reproduce without permission.

£upercasinos

The proposal to create supercasinos was not one of those subjects that caused a flurry of commentary, but rather a steady stream of disapproval from the time the idea was introduced in late 2005 to when Gordon Brown became Prime Minister and killed off the idea in the summer of 2007.

Between January 2007 and January 2008 there were 57 columns of commentary about supercasinos, many in the early part of the year comparing Blackpool and Manchester, both towns considered suitable sites by the government for a supercasino.

Nick Cohen was in a waspish mood in The Observer (January 14) when he looked towards Australia as an example of how governments become as addicted to the potential tax revenues of gambling – 'Of all the addictions gambling fuels, the one we should fear most is the dependency of governments. Once they are hooked, it takes a tremendous effort to wrench them free.' He observed that the internet had created a culture which meant that gambling can take place at anytime and anywhere which in turn meant that the government wouldn't have to feel that all gambling problems would be laid at the door of casinos. What he wanted was an admission from ministers 'that gambling must be contributing to the debt which is sinking so many households.' [21]

On January 30 2007 the government announced plans for 17 new casinos with one super or 'regional' casino in Manchester. On the same day the then culture secretary Tessa Jowell answered questions in the House of Commons. She responded to Conservative MP Julie Kirkbride's concerns about the effects of gambling on those families who could least afford it by echoing Nick Cohen's predictions of what the government response would be.

"On the point about deep social change, that social change is going on anyway. Every single television and mobile phone, as well as the internet, offers opportunities for gambling which were not available even five years ago. The Government are committed to public protection through legislation that protects the vulnerable, but we recognise that millions of people want to gamble as a legitimate leisure pursuit and should be allowed to do so." (Hansard publications January 30 2007)[22]

For the majority of columnists writing about the issue supercasinos became the symbol of the government's greed and lack of morality. Martin Townsend in The Daily Express on February 14 wrote that he was 'horrified' about the plans for Manchester [23], (the Daily Express and its columnists were the supercasino's most vocal critics) In March in the Daily Mail Max Hastings, called for Tessa Jowell's resignation because of her immorality[24] and in the same month (27th) Polly

[21] Nick Cohen, The Observer, 14th January 2008. [22] Hansard Publications, 30th January 2008. [23] Martin Townsend, The Daily Express, 14th February 2007. [24] Max Hastings, The Daily Mail, 27th March 2007. Copyright Editorial Intelligence Ltd 2008. Do not reproduce without permission.

Toynbee of The Guardian worried about the effect on the families of gambling addicts.[25] Most seemed to feel that there would be better ways to regenerate an area than to put a great big casino on it.

These outraged voices didn't seem to be soothed by Gordon Brown's 2007 budget which imposed a penal rate of taxation on casinos and announced a tax on online gambling operations designed to discourage sites from registering in the United Kingdom. There were only a few commentators who didn't share the pack's disapproval. A notable exception was Daniel Finkelstein, comment editor of The Times, writing on March 28 in reaction to the House of Lords rejection that day of the supercasino in Manchester. Finkelstein felt that Britain had a long history of 'panics about gambling' and went back to the time of Elizabeth I when the first ever lottery provoked the 'outrage' by leaders of the respectable middle-class opinion' who

just couldn't bear to see 'rewards allocated through sheer luck to the feckless and indolent'. Finkelstein had a dig at the distaste of the left, in the form of another commentator, Polly Toynbee, who had written the day before about supercasinos and ended with a blast at City bonuses, people buying yachts and 'global-finance gambles with their aura of corrupting unreality'. For Toynbee, Finkelstein wrote, it might be difficult to stop such squalid and unmerited booty but at least there was something that could be done to stop casinos.

Finkelstein felt that this saving people from themselves attitude was both patronising and futile, and that most restriction only ends in the habit or pastime thriving underground – 'The idea that one supercasino in Manchester is going to undermine the foundations of a civilised society is ridiculous and immature. Tessa Jowell's position is brave and right. Now she needs a little luck. I

Commentary on Supercasinos from Jan 2007-Jan 2008

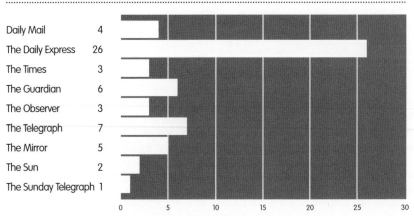

Daily Mail	4
The Daily Express	26
The Times	3
The Guardian	6
The Observer	3
The Telegraph	7
The Mirror	5
The Sun	2
The Sunday Telegraph	1

[25] Polly Toynbee, The Guardian, 27th March 2007. Copyright Editorial Intelligence Ltd 2008. Do not reproduce without permission.

hope she gets it.'[26] Less then a month after he became Prime Minister Gordon Brown chose to tell parliament his 'moral compass' led him to believe that regeneration might be a better way of meeting [the] economic and social needs of deprived areas than a Las Vegas-style casino. Whitehall sources later acknowledged that the controversial plans were "dead in the water".[27] Well, not quite, on February 26 the government stated that they still had plans to build 16 smaller casinos. The Daily Mail leader on hearing rumours of the plans in January had asked Mr Brown to 'think again' and to search around for that famous moral compass [28] while Polly Toynbee rolled up her sleeves for a new fight against the 'perverse logic of the industry's commitment to something called "socially responsible gambling". While she didn't suggest banning gambling she felt that there was an important social difference between adults doing what they pleased to thrusting it at them in everyday life. She urged parliament to vote against what would still be Britain's 'biggest ever casinos'[29].

The Gurkhas

Much of the commentary about the plight of Gurkhas denied the right to settle in Britain because they retired before 1997 came after the Gurkhas protested at the House of Commons, with the Liberal Democrat leader Nick Clegg becoming their very visible political champion.

Vicki Woods, however, wrote about the Gurkhas difficult situation in The Daily Telegraph of June 30. This was something which many people felt had been resolved in September 2004 when the government confirmed that it would change immigration rules to let them stay, she wrote, but there was a loop-hole which meant that only Gurkhas who had served for at least four years and who had been discharged after July 1 1997 were eligible for 'fast-track' citizenship. She highlighted the efforts of the Army Rumour Service website (ARRSE) which was trying to actively publish other cases of Gurkhas being treated unfairly.[30] Carole Malone was quick off the mark too when on August 5 she wrote in the Sunday Mirror that it would be a 'supreme gesture of goodwill to allow them to spend their last years here.'[31]

By late summer the Daily Express had started a 'Support the Gurkas' text campaign and the paper could rightly claim in March that it had long been the most active supporter of Gurkhas' rights with constant news stories in the previous six months by Martyn Brown, dozens of

[26] Daniel Finkelstein, The Times, 28th March 2007. [27] Whitehall sources, BBC Nnews 24, 11th July 2007. [28] Leader, The Daily Mail, 23rd January 2008. [29] Polly Toynbee, The Guardian, 26th February 2008. [30] Vicki Woods, The Daily Telegraph, 30th June 2007. [31] Carole Malone, the Sunday Mirror, 5th August 2007. Copyright Editorial Intelligence Ltd 2008. Do not reproduce without permission.

letters from outraged readers and leaders on the subject on March 19, 20 and 26. The plight of the Gurkhas was used as a launch pad to discuss immigration in general by The Daily Express and The Daily Mail. The Daily Express leader of March 26 said: "Even murderers and rapists could be entitled to a British passport if their homeland was considered "too dangerous" under human rights laws for them to be deported. In Labour's morally deprived universe, more "rights" accrue to murderers and rapists than brave, law-abiding Gurkhas such as Falklands war hero Gyanendra Rai, who has been denied NHS treatment for back injuries that nearly killed him."[32]

Sarah Sands' commentary in The Independent on Sunday was particularly powerful, because of the extremely moving quality of her commentary. It was soon picked up by bloggers and pro-Gurkhas websites. She compared the dignity , honour and bravery of the Gurkhas to the tawdry case of Raymond Horne, an elderly paedophile who arrived in Britain having been kicked out of Australia with his British citizenship intact. She pointed out that Prince Harry was put under the care of the Gurkhas and spoke of meeting many Gurkhas when she was in Afghanistan last August. Sands described the friendships she developed: 'As I sat quietly with my guide watching the sun set over the Himalyas, I felt the pull of historical ties and shared values. The Gurkhas are among Britain's oldest allied and deepest friends.'[33]

---

[32] Leader, The Daily Express, 26th March. [33] Sarah Sands, The Independent on Sunday, 23rd March 2008. Copyright Editorial Intelligence Ltd 2008. Do not reproduce without permission

"Political reputations are yo-yoing and columnists are like a herd of wildebeest – it's bedlam. More like power of the madhouse than power of the Commentariat" – Nick Cohen

AA Gill, 18
Aaronovitch, David, 17, 19, 24
Adam Smith Institute, 30
Adrian Monck, 30
Adonis, Andrew, 10
Allan, Richard, 30
Alexander, Wendy. 30
Ashley, Jackie, 7, 27
Audiotheque, 30
BAA, 39
Balls, Ed , 26, 27, 36
Bank of England, 35, 37
BBC, 13, 16, 17, 20, 29, 43
BBC Internet Blog, 30
Beau Beau d'Or, 30
Bernstein, Carl, 25
Biased BBC, 30
Bill Thompson, 30
Blackhurst, Chris, 36
Blair , Ian, 25
Blair, Cherie, 32
Blair, Tony, 10, 12, 13, 23, 24, 25, 26, 27, 32
Blunkett, David, 25
Branson, Richard, 34, 36
Brassneck, 17, 20, 22, 30
Bright, Martin, 22, 30, 31
British Press Awards, 18
Brogan, Ben, 17, 30
Broken TV, 30
Brown, Gordon, 12, 13, 19, 24, 27, 31, 33, 34, 36, 40, 41, 42
Brown, Tina, 20, 21, 22, 24, 29
Brown, Martyn, 43
Brummer, Alex, 36
Byers, Stephen, 25
Cabinet Office, 8
Cameron, David, 9, 12, 20
Campbell, Alastair, 26
Carr, Simon, 12
Cavendish, Camilla, 39
CBI, 24
City of Sound, 30
Channel4FactCheck, 30
Clarke, Charles, 11, 12, 17, 18, 23, 25
Clarkson, Jeremy, 17, 22, 29

Clegg, Nick, 43
Clinton, Bill, 31
Clinton, Hilary, 24
Cohen, Nick, 9, 17, 21, 22, 24, 28, 30, 41, 44
Cohen, Omerli, 23
Comment Central, 17
Comment is Free, 17, 31
Competition Commission, 11
Connor, Alan, 20, 29, 30
ConservativeHome, 31
Conservative Party, 36
Cridland, James, 30
Currybet, 30
d'Ancona, Matthew, 16, 19
Dacre, Paul, 21
Daily Mail, The, 9, 10, 14, 16, 17, 18, 20, 21, 22, 26, 32, 35, 36, 37, 38, 40, 41
Daily Express, The, 37, 40, 41, 43, 44
Daily Mirror, 26
Daily Telegraph, The, 8, 16, 17, 18, 20, 24, 37, 43
Dale , Iain, 17, 30, 31
Daley, Janet, 24, 26
Darling, Alastair, 35, 36, 37
Davies, Evan, 30
Davies, Will, 30
Dispatches, Channel Four, 22, 30
Drudge, Matt, 30, 31
Economist, The, 24
Editorial Intelligence, 11, 15, 18
Electorial Commission, 30
EMC Media Blog, 30
Equality and Human Rights Commission, 23
European Exchange Rate Mechanism, 11
Evan Davies, 30
Evening Standard, 9, 12, 16, 17, 36, 39
Facebook, 15
Farndon, Lucy, 36
Fawkes, Guido, 17, 31
Fealty, Mick, 20, 22, 30
Financial Times, 9, 10, 11, 12,

16, 17, 18, 20, 24, 25, 28, 36
Finkelstein, Daniel, 17, 42
Fischer, Joschka, 30
Fox, George, 7
Freedland, Jonathan, 17, 31
FSA, 35
Garton Ash, Timothy, 10, 12, 25, 29
Goldman Sachs, 38
Goldsmith, Zac, 39
Gove, Michael, 26
Green, Michael, 23
Greenslade, Roy Professor, 17, 30
Guardian, The, 7, 10, 12, 16, 17, 18, 19, 20, 23, 24, 25, 27, 29, 30, 31, 36, 37, 40, 42
Grove, Michael, 26
Guido Fawkes, 30
Gyford, Phil, 30
Halligan, Liam, 37
Hamilton, Adrian, 37
Hansard, 26, 41
Harry's Place, 30
Hastings, Sir Max, 41
Hain, Peter, 17, 30
Heathrow, 39, 40
Heffer, Simon, 24
Hello, 32
Hilton, Anthony, 19
Hitchens, Christopher, 30
Hitchens, Peter, 9, 28
Horne, Raymond, 44
Hutton, Will, 17
Independent, The, 12, 22, 23, 28, 37
James, Howell, 8, 13, 14, 23, 25, 26, 29
Jenkins, Simon, 16, 19, 22, 28, 39
Johnson, Andrew, 37
Johnson, Boris, 12, 18, 19
Johnson , Rachel, 11, 28
Jowell, Tessa, 40, 41, 42
Kaletsky, Anatole, 16, 24
Kavanagh, Trevor, 8, 16, 22
Kellaway, Lucy, 18
Kelly, John, 22

Kennedy, Caroline, 13
Kennedy, Charles, 19
Kettle, Martin, 24
Kim Dale's Diary, 30
King, Justin, 12
Kingsmill, Denise, 10, 11, 14
Kirkbride, Julie, 41
Klein, Joe, 30
Lambert, Richard, 24
Lewinsky, Monica, 31
Liddle, Rod, 22, 35
Littlejohn, Richard, 8, 14, 16, 22, 35
Livingstone, Ken, 12, 19, 22
Lost remote, 30
MacShane, Denis, 11, 14, 18, 22, 25, 27, 29, 30
Maguire, Kevin, 25
Mail on Sunday, 9, 23
Major, John, 11, 24
Make My Vote Count, 30
Malone, Carole, 43
Mandelson, Peter, 25
Mardell, Mark, 30
Mark Mardell, 30
Martin, Iain, 9, 24, 25, 31
Martin Moore, 30
McCartney, Sir Paul, 29
McElvoy, Anne, 16
Meyer, Catherine, 13, 17, 29, 30
Meyer, Sir Christopher, 11, 23, 27
Miliband, David, 12, 24
Mills, Heather, 29
Mirror Group Newspapers, 28
Monbiot, George, 16, 25
Montgomerie, Tim, 31
Moore, Martin, 30
Moore, Suzanne, 9, 23
Murdoch, Rupert, 8
My Right Wing Dad, 30
Naughton, John, 20
News of the World, 12, 17, 27
Nelson , Fraser, 27
New Statesman, 22, 31
New Yorker, 20
Nixon, Richard, 25

Normblog, 30
Norman, Matthew, 18
Northern Rock, 35, 38
Number 10, 11
Obama, Barrack, 34
Oblomovka, 30
Oborne, Pete, 8, 9, 18, 19, 20, 27, 38
Observer, The, 9, 12, 17, 27, 31, 41
Open democracy, 30
OrderOrder, 31
Osborne, George, 12
Parris, Matthew, 18
Penn, Mark, 24
Peston, Robert, 16, 17, 27, 30
Phil Gyford, 30
Phillips, Melanie, 8, 9, 10, 20, 21, 22, 27, 29, 31
Phillips, Trevor, 23
PoliticsHome, 31
Popieluszko, Jerzy, 12
Porter, Henry, 12
Potlatch, 30
Pratley, Nils, 36, 37
Prescott, John, 31
Press Complaints Commission, 11, 23
Prospect, 21, 22, 30
Rachman, Gideon, 9, 20
Rai, Gyanendra, 44
Randall, Jeff, 16
Rawnsley, Andrew, 27, 31
Redbox, 17, 30
Reuters Institute, 12
Richards, Steve, 22, 28
Riddell, Mary, 8, 21, 27
Riddell, Peter, 13, 17, 22, 27, 28
Rifkind, Malcolm, 12
Robinson, Nick, 16, 17, 30
Russell, William, 25
RSA, 13
Samizdata, 30
Sands, Sarah, 44
Seymour, David, 28
Shakespeare, Stefan, 31
Sky News, 17

Slugger O'Toole, 20, 22
Spectator, The, 16, 27, 32
Stephens, Philip, 24, 25
Steinem, Gloria, 13
Stelzer, Irwin, 16
Stern , Stefan, 9, 11, 28
Story Curve, 30
Steven Berlin Johnson, 30
Sullivan, Andrew, 30
Supercasinos, 41
Sun, The, 16, 17, 23, 32, 39
Sunday Mirror, 43
Sunday Telegraph, The, 16, 17, 19
Sunday Times, The, 16, 17, 18, 19, 22, 28, 29, 36. 39, 40
Taylor, Matthew, 13, 22, 25, 26
Telegraph Media Group, 9, 24
Thatcher, Margaret, 23
Three Line Whip., 30
Times, The, 13, 16, 17, 18, 19, 22, 24, 26, 27, 28, 30, 39, 42
Tomski, 30
Townsend, Martin, 41
Toynbee, Polly, 8, 10, 14, 19, 20, 22, 24, 27, 35, 41, 42
Treasury Select Committee, 37
TreeHouse Trust, 14, 31
Vanity Fair, 12, 20
Walsh, Willie, 42
Watching TV Online, 30
Washington Post, 25
Whelan, Charlie, 13, 27
Williams, Rowan, 25
Winner, Michael, 18
Wolf, Martin, 10, 16, 18, 20
Wolfe, Tom, 23
Woods, Vicki, 43
Woodward, Bob, 25
Wylie, Ian, 14, 31
YouGov, 31
Young, Hugo, 18
York, Peter, 14, 23, 24